PENGUIN BOOKS
The Rugby Post

Kevyn Male was born in Te Kuiti, King Country, on 1 April 1943. From the age of five, until seventeen, he experienced life in the confines of two country stores that were owned and operated by his parents 'Jock and Daize'. In 1966 he opened his own store (The 3 Bears) on Broadway, Newmarket and thirty-four years down the track he still retails (Route 66) from the same location.

Kevyn's ability to take risks and stay ahead of the bunch has been crucial to his success as a fashion entrepreneur and today he firmly believes in doing whatever excites him the most.

Rugby has always been a passion of Kevyn's and he entered the senior ranks in 1961 as an eighteen-year-old member of the Otahuhu Club. He counts himself privileged to have played alongside the likes of Waka Nathan and Mac Herewini, and was an Auckland rugby representative from 1962–72.

Kevyn has published a number of books over the past fifteen years. *The Rugby Post* is his second book for Penguin this year.

On a personal front, he has strong interests in community affairs and the arts, especially sculpture and contemporary New Zealand painting and literature.

ACKNOWLEDGEMENTS

My special thanks to Mark Ryan (photography) for his skill in rescuing many difficult shots. And well done to my old, but reliable, Pentax Zoom 70. To the numerous garage proprietors, publicans, pub patrons, club secretaries and the kids on the street, my special thanks for poking me in the right direction to ensure I finished the job on time.

REFERENCE MATERIAL — ACKNOWLEDGEMENTS

The greater majority of the content printed in this book was sourced personally by the author. For the additional reference material supplied, my thanks and acknowledgements to the following:

- John McCullough and the Auckland Rugby Union

- The New Zealand Rugby Union

- Andy Haden, Murray Deaker and Kevin Lewis

. . . and to the numerous club secretaries and individual rugby enthusiasts who responded to the call.

The Rugby Post

Rugby's place in heartland New Zealand

Kevyn Male

PENGUIN BOOKS

PENGUIN BOOKS

Penguin Books (NZ) Ltd, cnr Airborne and Rosedale Roads, Albany,
Auckland 1310, New Zealand
Penguin Books Ltd, 27 Wrights Lane, London W8 5TZ, England
Penguin USA, 375 Hudson Street, New York, NY 10014, United States
Penguin Books Australia Ltd, 487 Maroondah Highway, Ringwood, Australia 3134
Penguin Books Canada Ltd, 10 Alcorn Avenue, Toronto, Ontario, Canada M4V 3B2
Penguin Books (South Africa) Pty Ltd, 5 Watkins Street, Denver Ext 4, 2094, South Africa
Penguin Books India (P) Ltd, 11 Community Centre, Panchsheel Park,
New Delhi 110 017, India

Penguin Books Ltd, Registered Offices: Harmondsworth, Middlesex, England

First published by Penguin Books (NZ) Ltd, 1999

1 3 5 7 9 10 8 6 4 2

Copyright © Kevyn Male, 1999

The right of Kevyn Male to be identified as the author of this work in terms of
section 96 of the Copyright Act 1994 is hereby asserted.

Typeset by Egan-Reid Ltd
Printed by Wyatt & Wilson Print Limited, Christchurch
Front cover: Teko, Bruce, David, and in front, 81-year-old George — Bulls Rugby Club.

CONTENTS

FOREWORD

In the course of my 40-year rugby playing career I have seen a fair few rural rugby grounds. Probably in fact a few more than most as my rural Wanganui origins offer a headstart in this area and I lay claim to being a bit of an expert in this domain.

If you drive through some of the smallest towns in New Zealand too quickly you wouldn't have any idea where the locals played their rugby on Saturday afternoons. Goal posts are usually the only giveaway that distinguishes the rugby paddock from other paddocks in the vicinity.

There is a pretty slim chance that the oil lines marking out the field will be visible until some bloke turns up with the lawnmower to 'tidy the show up', and if the mower man is also in the team, there is a chance he will assist even further by kicking some of the excess cow shit off the field as well. The sheep shit is left alone because it's good for a healthy grass growth!

The rural rugby bloke doesn't usually bother too much about having a shower after the game so changing sheds aren't essential. The back of the Landrover is as good a place as any to leave your clothes, i.e., unless the dogs chew the backside out of your strides while you're doing your best for the local XV.

Now that's not to say that there aren't some pretty flash clubrooms around the rural regions. Some have even got hot water and others can be as elaborate as providing a couple of lights along one side for training. Most don't go in for training though others cheat a bit in the training light department by angling a street light or a parked ute's headlights towards a corner of the ground where the greatest amount of nocturnal activity is expected to take place.

Some grandstands have been constructed on top of the changing sheds and more often than not nesting birds will have shit all over the place to complicate matters even further.

Raetihi's rugby paddock is in the middle of the showgrounds and is set amongst a maze of small pens and painted rails. If you don't know exactly the right way into the ground and park in the wrong place you end up having to jump more fences than they do in the local steeplechase.

Horrock's Park at Kaiwhaiki on the Whanganui River features a real flash changing-room affair — heaps of corrugated iron which seems to be the staple diet for a majority number of rural rugby facilities in New Zealand.

What goes on the tour stays on tour, and my apologies to the '99 Taihape Senior B's for Kevyn pulling the plug on publishing your recent team photo — more's the pity! Move on — she's a good read!

Andy Haden

INTRODUCTION

Like most kids in New Zealand, I was introduced to our national game at a very young age. I have vivid memories of owning my first rugby ball at six years of age and every now and again, Mum would give me some mutton fat to preserve it and I'd idolise it even further.

At ten, I owned my first pair of boots, a real heavy number, with big leather sprigs, which in later years the ref prudently inspected (pre-game) for the nail tips which popped up now and again through normal wear and tear.

Nothing too much transpired in my early winter mid-week days at Howick District High School, and much the same for the Saturday effort with the Howick Rugby Club. We rarely won a game!

This soon changed, however, with a switch to Otahuhu and at the very young age of seventeen, I found myself playing alongside two of my earlier rugby idols — Waka Nathan and the mercurial Mac Herewini.

A couple of years with the Auckland Colts followed, then it was an in and out affair for eight years with the Auckland As. During the 60s and 70s, when your time was up with Auckland representative rugby, the Union had an arrangement whereby they said 'thanks but no thanks' and you got pensioned off with an end-of-season trip with the B team. I said sayonara by captaining the Bs on a jaunt to the Bay of Islands in 1972.

I've felt honoured to have met some wonderful New Zealanders during the compiling of this book. The most notable observation, however, has been the re-emergence of the game in the rural provinces, with prominent gains being achieved in the East Coast, Taranaki/Manawatu, Nelson Bays, the West Coast, Southland, Central and North Otago. I purposely left the main centres alone, largely because I felt they too often forget the true benefits of the game; the camaraderie, the humour and the rugby club as the main focal point of small communities and the grass roots of the game in New Zealand.

I've discovered hidden treasures in Waihou Bay, Waverley, Kohukohu, Collingwood, Karamea, Danseys Pass and the Catlins. These places have a strong sense of identity and residents are extremely loyal to their communities.

The message of this book? Not only is rugby our national game, it has often been the saviour by virtue of its status as the focal point of small communities in the regional areas of New Zealand.

So to all of those who have contributed to this book, I say thank you. We live in a great country, and as with the game, let us all help each other to preserve it.

I trust the enjoyment gained from the reading of this book is equal to the enjoyment of having put it together.

Kevyn Male

August 1999

The North

**Those
long tall
goal posts**

TALL GOAL POSTS are fairly frequently on show in the far north, and no field in New Zealand has got within a 'bull's roar' than the two sets currently on show at Kohukohu Domain in the Hokianga. And rest assured the likes of former North Auckland goal kicking greats such as Muru Walters, Victor Yates and the Going brothers, slotted a few more through as a result of the height of the posts at Whangarei's Rugby Park.

WELL! HE SURE LOOKS THE PART

The flip side of having tall goal posts on show is that they seem to get a touch of the 'bends' here and there.

Kohukohu, Hokianga
28 metres from
ground level
to the top

KOHUKOKU

KOHUKOHU MAKES NO claim to having the greatest team in the north, but they do claim to have the highest goal posts in Australasia, and I think they may be right! The posts are 28 metres from ground level to the top. The grandstand has seen better days but a field none the less with a proud history. The gates of remembrance proudly acknowledge dozens of locals who gave their lives for King and Country during the 1914–18 and 1939–45 World Wars.

So symbolic for North Auckland rugby supremacy during the 50s and 60s — tall kauri goal posts, the winter mud and a partisan crowd that backed their team to the hilt.

Rural rugby — a cockie's paddock, makeshift posts, and
sheep grazing to keep the grass down.

PUHOI DOMAIN

Puhoi was founded in 1865. My home town of fifty years ago is only 15 kilometres up the road — Ahuroa. Familiar territory for me as a kid, and likewise for the Brooke boys who went to the same school.

Did you know . . . ?
The first rugby match in New Zealand was officially played at Nelson in 1870.

Having a mid-day smack with the ball and the kids at Waipu Primary.

Northern rural rugby — steel goal posts and horses keeping the grass in order plus gate boxes with a clear message for law and order.

THE JONES BOY — 'TIGER'

PETER JONES REPRESENTED New Zealand over a seven-year period, 1953–1960. He first represented North Auckland as an 18-year-old and graduated to a North Island reserve later in the same year. Renowned for playing the game hard but clean, Peter was proud of the fact that he was never ordered off a rugby field. I once had the memorable experience of playing with him and against him in Barbarian Sunday charity matches during the early 60s — I much preferred the former! Peter is best remembered for his wonderful 56 fourth test opportunist try that both clinched the game and the series for the All Blacks against the Springboks, and then post match, grabbing the microphone and announcing to the nation and the rugby world that he was absolutely 'buggered'. He died in 1994 at the age of 62.

Unique — Pangatotara on the road to Murchision. A private back-road field and posts featuring a unique style 3 x 2 post extension. I'd be confident in saying it's a oncer for New Zealand.

Posts and Profiles

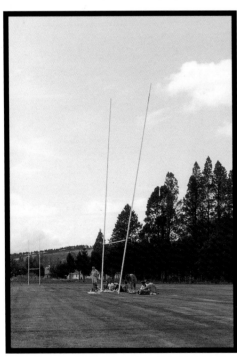

A touch of the leans — Rangatira Club (Gisborne), Bombay Primary and Waiouru Military Camp.

One – Two – Three

Top left to right: A pre-season common sight – a solitary post; an Opotiki school field showing no bias between soccer and rugby.

Left: Waitai Domain on the coast between Dunedin and Palmerston. A three-in-one affair, a joint ground usage between rugby and the A & P Association might explain it.

A Mixed Bag

Left to right: Pine posts, steel bar and 3 x 2 extensions, Catlins region Southland; a real fat affair (Wanganui Basin) which also dubs as a firehose drying facility for the local brigade; one up one down — rural King country, and the too hard basket, repairing the sunken post padding and the bit the mower missed.

Rural Jobs

Clockwise from top left: South Waikato farm that promotes a return for two parties — the farmer and the local rugby enthusiasts; East Coast, a real back-of-beyond job with a post that had sprung some fresh growth at its tip; Kieran, Timmy and Angus in front of the posts, Glenorchy Primary, Queenstown region; and a standard equipment set for junior school grounds — 200mm round tanalised posts and a 4 x 2 crossbar, Western Bay, Lake Taupo.

Seen Better Days

A 'had-its-day' rural ground ticket box, Northland; a long-forgotten ground turnstyle, Southland; and from Ugaere School, Taranaki, a piece of 'Kiwi Kids' humour. 'A few of us were swinging on the crossbar and we pulled the bugger down.'

Central

Bulls Rugby Club is one of the oldest rugby clubs in New Zealand (123 years) and part of the Manawatu Rugby Union. Pictured here are Teko, Bruce, David and in front, the club's pride and joy, 81-year-old caretaker George.

GEORGE THIRD

Eighty-one-year-old George Third, caretaker of the Bulls Rugby Club ground and clubrooms, is one of those rugby stalwarts most clubs would die for. Single baggage man-cum spare tyre for the Bulls Golden Oldies team, he last took the field in Canada for the 1998 world competition. A former hooker by trade, he's bred four sons and two daughters, and all four boys have played for Bulls at some stage during the last thirty years.

TAIRUA RUGBY CLUB

Rugby football first came to Tairua in the early 1880s. The main opponent in those days was Mercury Bay and according to legend, part of the deal was a three-day bush walk to wage battle on the field over the hill. A day's rugby on the local patch at Tairua often started with a horse ride from Hikuai to Tairua or from the opposite direction, Whenuakite and Coroglen.

Prior to the Second World War, with an expanded competition in place, players assembled at Tairua and were sent by boat to Whitianga where they were met by an old flat-top truck and driven down the road to Kuaotunu to play the game.

The first rugby field at Tairua was the paddock between the school and the hotel. It was moved 80 years ago to its present site which in its early days also doubled as a racetrack. The ground was given to the community of Tairua by an early rugby enthusiast, Harold Cory-Wright.

In front of the posts, all the sevens — the three seventy-seven-year old life members of the club, Jim Farley, Allan Beach and Reg Laycock.

THE WAVERLEY CONNECTION

KIWI — WITH SNOW LUPTON ON BOARD

THE WAVERLEY CLUB claims to be one of the oldest registered rugby clubs in New Zealand. It's also the home territory of the famous racehorse 'Kiwi' trained by Snow Lupton. We all saw Jimmy Cassidy guiding Kiwi home from last at the last turn to win the 1983 Melbourne Cup. What we didn't see was Snow and his wife Anne (all dressed up in her raceday hat) trucking Kiwi personally to the track, and following the win, Snow trucking him home again to his Melbourne quarters in preference to arriving on time for the official post-race dinner.

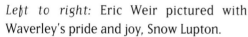

Left to right: Eric Weir pictured with Waverley's pride and joy, Snow Lupton.

Eric's been a true 'nuts and bolts' performer (where would the game be without them) for the past fifty years on the grass-roots circles of Taranaki rugby.

One-Game Henry (left of top right picture) attended his one and only rugby game over fifty years ago at Tongaporutu on a South Taranaki rugby paddock. He didn't like what he saw and hasn't played or seen (including TV) a rugby game since.

Right: George (Izzie) Isbister, 83. A legend in the Waverley region, Izzie according to some more 'good oil' has dealt to a few on and off the field. A former bushman cum jack-of-all-trades, he started one Wanganui rep game on the flank but quickly moved into the front row to warm the boys up a little! He's tackled most medical problems with a dose of castor oil, or would you believe, a similar-sized dose of diesel.

TAIHAPE — GUMBOOT TERRITORY

Everybody's got a pair of gumboots but Taihape seems to own more than most.

Taihape is unquestionably the gumboot and number-eight-wire capital of the world. I caught the boys a bit early at Taihape — the posts weren't up. In front of the scoreboard, Austin (club patron), Bill and Dave with wirecutters, the number-eight and their gumboots in tow.

The rural 'grandstand'. Similar to many other small rugby centres in New Zealand, Taihape owns a real 'beauty'!

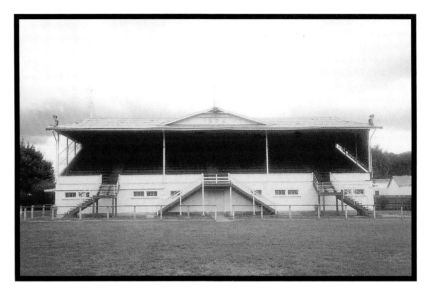

WHAREPAPA SOUTH — SOUTH WAIKATO

Country style, tanalised posts, 4 x 2 crossbar, a rough paddock, a no-frills long-drop, and left and right the user unfriendly 'scrum machine'.

Similar to Taihape, too early and not a rugby post to be seen in Ohakune, but plenty of carrots and gumboots according to a local stalwart Rex Oliver.

The goal shall consist of two upright posts, 5.6 metres apart, joined by a crossbar, the lower face of which shall be 3 metres from ground level. That's what the rule book says, but on my reckoning a large majority of New Zealand rugby posts on show have ended up with a measurement all of their own.

A blast from the past! The rural rugby ground 'long drop'.

Bums on Seats

BUMS ON SEATS

The Score-keepers

Left to right: Waiouru — high chair cum scoreboard and Reefton, Murchison and Ranfurly — keeping the score and satisfying the sponsors.

Provincial Rugby Ground Grandstands

Top left: Hunterville. *Middle left:* Motueka. *Bottom left:* Greymouth. B*elow:* Marton, Sanson.

A favoured facility for the rugby silent majority – closer to the game and a style and flavour all of their own. Fine examples of provincial rugby grandstands.

For the record books (but since rectified), the Hunterville Domain was home to a rugby field that sloped so much that a crossbar at one end was level with the ground level between the posts at the other end – a slope of nine feet!

Kumara — West Coast

Unquestionably not attracting the crowds of old, and going by the position of the scrum machine poked in the blackberries behind the main stand, the Kumara seniors don't much favour that side of the game either!

Seats for bums

The rural ticket box and the highly original rural 'dunnies' of the 50s and 60s.

Heath Robinson

Heath Robinson, and unquestionably past their 'use-by' date, clockwise from top right — Northland dunny and East Coast and Taihape seen-better-days scrum machines.

. . . and — bums in the air

Taihape and Inglewood putting the brakes on with water-filled 44s, and the Central Otago boys settling the same business with some good old-fashioned concrete!

Seen better days — New Zealand rural rugby 'long drops', two from the North and two from the South.

The unsung heroes of the
game — referees, coaches
and linesmen. No sitting
down at half-time in my day,
that is unless you were
leading by 30 points!

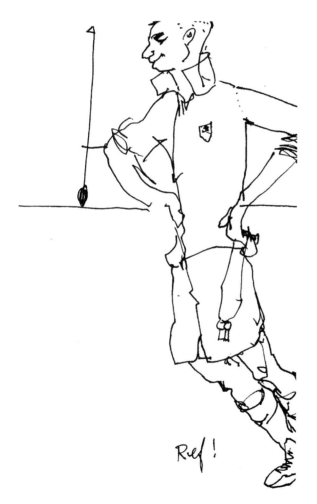

Ref!

and more bums . . .

The East Coast

The last post . . .
Martyn Peat, a former East Coast rep,
paying homage to a long-forgotten,
solitary East Coast rugby post.

5 THE EAST COAST

Tikitiki School

As per the signpost — the heart and soul regions for East Coast rugby.

Right: I missed a set of unique New Zealand goal posts on the East Coast by a matter of months. George Raroa, the groundsman at Tikitiki School, told me they had just removed New Zealand's classic set of goal posts — two 25-year-old poplar trees.

WHAREKAHIKA SCHOOL, HICKS BAY

Above: This two-teacher school, including headmaster Komene Campbell, was founded in 1887. The Friday school assembly (role 32) was preceded by this shot in front of the goal posts. *Above right:* Hicks Bay — post training night, a real family affair. *Bottom right:* Sponsoring the game — Lion, DB and Speights have a majority hold elsewhere, but Tui's obviously an acquired taste around here.

The immortal
George Nepia
– his record
speaks for itself.

GEORGE NEPIA

Born 25 April 1905 in Wairoa, died 27 August 1986 in Ruatoria.

George represented New Zealand from 1924 to 1930. He played 46 matches for the All Blacks including 9 tests and scored 1 try, 39 conversions, 6 penalty goals. Nepia reached the pinnacle of his rugby career during the famous Invincibles tour of Great Britain (1924–25) where he took the field in all of the thirty matches played. In 1935–37 he switched codes to play rugby league in England. After being reinstalled back into rugby Nepia appeared twice more (at the age of 42) for East Coast. Aged 45, George played his last first-class game against a Poverty Bay team that was captained by his son, George junior.

Bob Scott and George Nepia

Bob Scott was born in 1921 and represented New Zealand in 52 matches from 1946 to 1954 playing in 17 tests. He was a prominent figure in the famous 1945 post-war 'Kiwi' services team and played in 19 of the 38 matches scoring 129 points. Bob Scott invariably brought a crowd to their feet every time he made contact with the ball. A 'dream' team member for those who played with him, but more of a nightmare for the opposition.

As a young kid, I had Bob Scott plastered all over my bedroom walls, and as a 13-year-old I was fortunate enough to see him play in a charity match for the Barbarians.

Waiapu Rugby Ground. The Waiapu community is proud of their favourite son, George Nepia, and equally so of their Maori heritage.

Te Puia School — East Coast. Te Puia is a small school, as is their 50-metre rugby field. A sow and some piglets were part of the deal when this photo was taken, the sow scuttling just prior to the photo.

AUCKLAND RUGBY FOLKLORE — MAD DOG MOORE

How does a guy get a name like Mad Dog Moore? In his day, Roger Moore was a very aggressive winger for Otahuhu and while still in his teens was called into service for the famous Queen Street Yanks who every two years took a holiday on the East Coast under the directorship of the equally famous Peter Hall. On one bus trip into the unknown, Moore stood up in the back of the bus and announced that he could smell pigs. Being so young, his statement was simply brushed aside. But five miles further on, the mob of pigs that blocked the road was so big, and the stench so great, that when the bus reached Ruatoria many of the Yanks were so crook that Hally (the coach) contemplated ringing ARU headquarters for more troops. Needless to say, Moore was immediately accepted as a fully paid-up member of the Yanks, and only one day after leaving Auckland. Full membership allowed a player a permanent space on the back seat of the bus. A true story based on factual evidence.

The true flavour of outback rugby on the East Coast. Ground and post conditions are of no major importance and nor for that matter is a whole 'heap' of scrum practice. According to Norman Boyton (Rangatira Club, north of Gisborne) their seniors don't exactly favour that side of the game either.

Marotiri School

In South Waikato they take their rugby fairly seriously. Marotiri School has a roll of 130 and none are more serious than these two twelve-year-olds — Wi Church and Michael Murphy. Their 10th-grade side won 17 out of 18 games in the 1998 10th-grade South Waikato competition. Super 12 stamped all over these two!

The Little Fellas

GLENBROOK SCHOOL

Barbara Duckworth is the dedicated principal of 254 pupils at Glenbrook Primary. The school rugby posts are of the standard school variety — pine posts with a steel crossbar.

POLLOCK AND INANGAHUA SCHOOLS

Above: It's back to basics at Pollock School, Manukau Heads (steel posts and bar) with a roll of just 35.

Above right: A shot of four of the kids (Inangahua School— roll 13) in front of their posts in the long grass. Great kids and fantastic surroundings in rural New Zealand away from the main centres. 'These are our posts and who cares if the bar's too low and the posts are too short.'

TOTARA FLAT SCHOOL—
SOUTH ISLAND

Going by his kicking style and his junior All Black jersey, young Duncan can't wait for the big stuff.

MURCHISON PRIMARY

Showtime for a few of the young stars in front of their school 'sticks'.

RIWAKA

All smiles in front of their school posts for six of the 'wee little fellas'.

KURATAU AND RIWAKA (MOTUEKA)

Situated on the south western side of Lake Taupo, Kuratau has a roll of 84 and the rugby players play in the Saturday Turangi-Taupo competition. A real country style set of posts – pine posts with a ti-tree crossbar held together with some galvanised wire. Pictured at showtime are Randall, six-year-old Richard, Glen and Nicholas.

INANGAHUA PRIMARY SCHOOL

Eleven of the kids of a school roll of 13 in front of their posts, the
long grass, and a short 50-metre field. Plus Dolly the dog!

WAITOTARA PRIMARY — SOUTH TARANAKI

Thomas Hill, an All Black prop of the future, pictured in front of his school pine posts and the legendary 4 x 2 crossbar. His dad Francis, a former Taranaki and Wanganui rep, runs the store across the road.

AHITITI SCHOOL

On the road towards Waitoetoe in North Taranaki. With a roll of only 13, the kids are given a choice on how best to score a goal. The star performers — Kelly, Jason and Ashley.

WHANGAPARAOA (EAST COAST), MOKAU AND RIWAKA

Right: This is a fine East Coast example of a shared rugby field for the little fellas and the big boys. Whetu Haerewa on show here with some youngsters behind what are arguably New Zealand's smallest set of goal posts. Whetu was the assistant coach for the East Coast team during the 1998 season.

Above left: Mokau School, on the coastal road towards New Plymouth. One short and one tall for the seen-better-days goal posts. Wyatt, Billy, Chris and Adam play their Saturday rugby in the Urenui competition.

Above right: Riwaka Primary — it wasn't a mufti day, but like most of Nelson and Tasman Bay, home to kids and adults with a wonderful outlook on life.

Flag Swamp School, fifty ks north of Dunedin (roll 13). A real 'doozie' this little rugby field and posts, and likewise with the lad doing the honours — eight-year-old Andrew Lee.

(To Neil Foot — special thanks K.M.)

Rugby Promoters

And none better than the likes of **Mad Dog Moore** (**NZ Barbarians**),
Saturday support crew, and the stars of the future — in this case,
New Windsor Primary.

Saturday Heroes

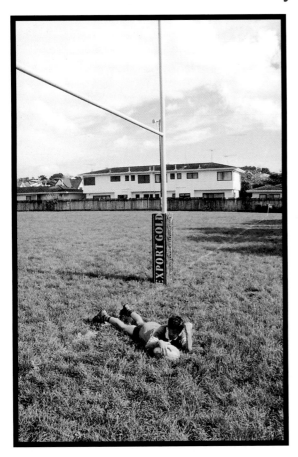

Above left: Coming up with the goods with a five-pointer under the bar — twelve-year-old Ryan Croawell, Pakuranga 7th grade 'Gold'. *Above right:* Support crew — Mum and the kids doing the 'rugby supporter' bit and the 'silent salesman' *(left)* coach wrapping up the game with a match post-mortem.

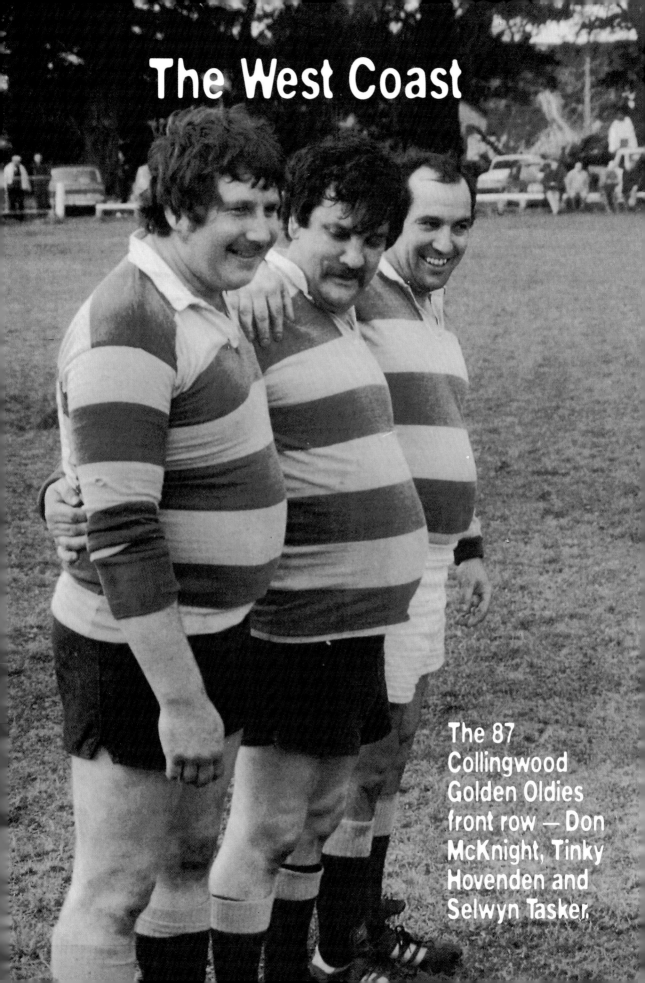

The West Coast

The 87 Collingwood Golden Oldies front row — Don McKnight, Tinky Hovenden and Selwyn Tasker.

THE COLLINGWOOD CONNECTION

ONE HUNDRED AND thirty kilometres west of Nelson and just south of the tip of the South Island (Farewell Spit) lies Collingwood. Their favourite rugby son, Todd Blackadder, has moved on to greater heights as the inspirational leader of the Canterbury Crusaders. Luckily, however, the area still abounds in rugby tales from past glory days and none better than the following from a current high country (all ten acres) sheep farmer.

Left: Jim (Wobbly) Weale has one son, Spare Weale, who's produced a few grandchildren for Wobbly — locally they're referred to as the Trolley Weales. Wobbly's sheep dog, Couzie-bro, has been upstaged of late by Wobbly and his wife in the mustering department. They throw a fishnet over the sheep just prior to the annual wool clip — all forty of them.

Unfortunately Wobbly's rugby career has followed a similar fate. In 1959, while in the Army in Wellington, Wobbly informed me that the 'good oil' had him shortlisted to represent the All Blacks against the 1959 Lions. A twenty-stone Maori prop soon put paid to that theory and he awoke two days later in Wellington Hospital and never set foot on a rugby paddock again. A rugby tale very similar to the fate of 'One-Game Henry' from Waverley!

Tinky Hovenden, proprietor of the Collingwood Hotel, had similar desires for All Black honours with the 1960 tour to South Africa. He has since settled his ambitions by becoming President of the 'Blackadder' fan club and the anchor inside back for the Collingwood Golden Oldies for the past twenty years.

Tall thick + intelligent !!

KARAMEA

Bob the caretaker (sports and rugby domain) with wife Jocelyn had just hung the washing out to dry in the small but cute grandstand. Home was a big articulated rig parked close by.

HOKITIKA

Andy Henderson and Wayne Stuart, stalwarts of the 'Golden Oldies' formulae on the West Coast, feature for the Kiwi Rugby Club in Hokitika. In their words '. . . the seniors hang around the middle of the pile at the end of a winter's competition'. Andy's rugby museum, on show in the top half of his house, is a rugby collector's dream. Young Wayne comes from the wild side of the tracks — a bushworker and fisherman from hell.

West Coast Legends

JOE (JUICY) SYRON — 59

Right: Juicy was a Buller rep from 1961–73, No. 8 in the 1960s, prop in the 70s. He dealt to a few rugby 'big shots' in his day including Andy Haden and the late Alistair Hopkinson. Up until last year, Juicy was still doing the business in the front row, but at a lower level and at a slower pace. A man of few words, Juicy lives at Waimangaroa on the road towards Karamea and milks a herd of 250 cows. He says its okay to be late for a wedding, a funeral, the bank manager or a Dairy Company meeting, but God help you if you're late for a rugby match! He's obviously quite keen on the game.

WESTPORT

Left: Jim Halsall, representative player for West Coast Buller from 1959–73. His career highlight was captaining the West Coast Buller Combined against the 1971 Lions in a game they lost 39–3. A true West Coaster with a smile to match.

KARAMEA

The seniors were fighting a losing battle for years, but last season they joined forces with Ngakawau down the road towards Westport, and their fortunes have turned around somewhat. Carl and Jack (shown here) don't actually know who rightfully owns the 'Burrows' Shield, but similar to much of the West Coast culture – it doesn't really matter!

Backyard jobs

King Country

A 'well-oiled' farm backyard job — King Country, north Taranaki region, and going by the No. 10 jersey on the line, home territory for a Grant Fox in the making.

TI-TREE STICK CLASSICS

Blue Hogg's two twelve-year-old grandsons, Tim and Liam Hogg, honing their rugby skills in front of their farm backyard job – Temuka.

And the Herbert's backyard – multi-purpose family affair at Omakau, Central Otago. Going by the TV aerials on show, they give the telly a real whack as well!

Mixed Bag

A backyard variety set in the house sheep paddock — Wanganui Basin.

Ruawai — in and amongst the bits and pieces of the cowshed paddock.

Coastal Taranaki — farm backyard job!

Top left: A backyard set of posts on a back country road heading towards Otorohanga. Home and target practice for nine-year-old Ashley McKain.

Right: A typical South Island primary school set of posts (round pine posts and a 4 x 2 crossbar) set on a three-quarter field – the Catlins, Southland.

Below: Two 'take-your-pick' (soccer and rugby) mobile arrangements – South Taranaki.

Mobile Backyard Job — Dunedin

Above: A Josh Kronfield of the future, only trouble being it's twelve-year-old Lauren Myers who plays her Saturday rugby for the Dunedin Rugby Club. Fifteen-year-old brother Richard was responsible for the mobile masterpiece which they move out onto the street when a more expansive game is required.

The youngest of Denise Keat's four boys, twelve-year-old Josh ready for a kicking session in front of their backyard cum backdoor job — 10 Galloway Street, Mornington, Dunedin.

The Loneliest Posts

The loneliest goal posts
in New Zealand —
Skippers Canyon,
Queenstown.

The notable aspect of this shot is the teenager leaning on the post — he is David Crotty, great-grandson of Charles John Munro who is officially attributed the honour of introducing the game of rugby into New Zealand in 1870. The game in question was between Nelson College and the Nelson Football Club and was played under full rugby rules on the Nelson Botanical Reserve.

Southern Man

Ed Pawsey with boots strung around his neck setting out for a training session at Fairlie — in the early 90s Ed travelled 1000km each week to play the game!

OWAKA

Owaka — true Southern rugby loyalists outside the local pub.
Kelly Chambers, Leadman (Ibby) Ibbotson and (how I never
made the All Blacks I'll never know) Bevan Smith.

Southern Pride

Flying high, a 'Southern Man' laying another line-out to rest.

A showcase small town rugby facility. In this case, the Queenstown Sports Centre going the whole nine yards for a pre-season Super 12 warm-up fixture, Hurricanes versus Highlanders.

WYNDHAM DOMAIN

'Waving the flag' in support of the local team: Tom, Debbie and Stu.

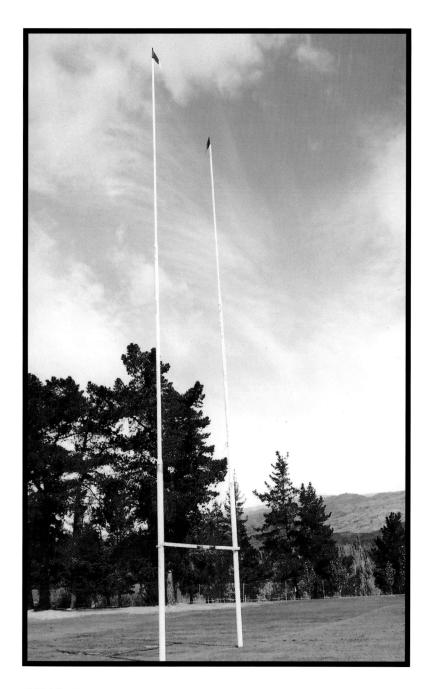

CLYDE

A local lad, Swooper, laid claim to their posts being the highest in the land. Sorry son, you're not even in the hunt. Kohukohu (Hokianga) has got 10 metres on you!

The Garston Connection

I'd never heard of Garston until I located Mrs Huffadine in the local pub. A real family affair with their private roadside field and rugby posts including the cat, dog, basketball hoop, and the rams.

Craig Chalmers in front of his personal posts, with his mate Matthew Huffadine. Craig and Matthew whipped me down to their old school (34 kids) to meet another star attraction in Garston — Michelle Malcolm the teacher.

P.S. My apologies Catherine for never having heard of Garston. As you say, it's not a problem for the Rawleigh's traveller, the Amway rep or the IRD.

SOPER BOYS TO THE RESCUE!

Sam Soper and his boys — George, Len, Davis, Clarence and Harold.

Post World War 1, Sam Soper (Athol, Southland) and his five boys well and truly surfaced when they came to the rescue of the Garston rugby team who could only muster eight players. Two more 'Athol' players were 'hooked' from an adjoining farm to play the major opposition of the day in Northern Southland (a team from Balfour) who were soundly defeated.

Sam and the boys lived at 'Riverview', Athol, beside the Mataura River. In front of their home was a horse paddock that for decades had been used as a fully equipped rugby field for matches played in the immediate area.

A.J. (Ack) Soper, an off-shoot of this tribe, represented Southland from 1954 to 1966 and reached the pinnacle of his rugby career by representing New Zealand as an All Black number eight for eight matches during 1957.

From the Author's Album

Left: Player of the day on his home ground — Horrocks Park, Wanganui. Big Andy pictured here walking off after the final whistle with 'Aunty Lucy' and his prize — a flax basket of pipis.

AMCO PLAYER OF THE DAY

Phill Gifford and yours truly introduced the 'Player of the Day' onto the rugby scene of Auckland during the late 1960s. Phill (aka Loosehead Len) chose the player from the main game and penned a few favourable comments in the *Rugby Weekly* the following week. Giving a player a pair of Amco Bull Denims (then $15) was at the time seriously questioned by the Rugby Union. 'Susan' of Herne Bay and Andy Haden and co, thankfully, soon put paid to the nonsense in the decade that followed.

BELIEVE IT OR NOT

In 1906 a rugby forward of sorts who played club rugby for Guys Hospital in England was invited by the Rugby Union to play a test match for England against the 1906/07 Springboks. His name was Dr Arnold Alcock and by all accounts he played a reasonable game in the test match which was played at Crystal Palace. The only trouble was that due to a typist's error he should not have taken the field in the first place. The invitation was meant for a Liverpool player with a similar name — L.A.N. Slocock. Slocock, in fact, went on to play eight further internationals for England.

Top: Andy Haden with his dog Jazz on the day he was picked as an All Black — aged 21.

Two of the greatest for putting the ball between the posts. *Below:* Auckland's Grant Fox and (*right*) Waikato's Don (the boot) Clarke.

Two Master Blasters

Three of the Greatest

Above: Bryan Williams — one of my two favourite rugby players to play with and against (the other being Waka Nathan). A long range goal-kicker to boot and an off-the-field credit to New Zealand rugby and Manu Samoa.

Left: Colin Meads — some say he was the greatest and they are most probably right.

Zin Zan Brooke in typical pose for Auckland — on the prowl and doing what he did best, scoring tries.

Hero Worship

Left: Fitzy and two of his young fans.

Right: Welsh rugby fanatic — John Walsh endorsing a favourable five-nation's result.

The ultimate: owning your own field

In this case a private affair — Pinnacle Hill, Bombay.

. . . and scoring (Paki Reihana) with a winning five-pointer under the bar.

The Rugby Bonus — mates for life!

'Different strokes for different blokes' as the saying goes, but for me the greatest rewards have come my way long after the game was over. In this case, two of my 60s Otahuhu mates Bill Kini and Waka Nathan — on the back of the truck, out at the farm, for the big '50'.

ARTIST ACKNOWLEDGEMENT

IT IS WITH SADNESS I RECORD THAT
THE ARTIST GARTH TAPPER WHO
DREW THE ILLUSTRATIONS IN THIS
BOOK PASSED AWAY SUDDENLY IN
APRIL, 1999.
K.M.